HAL LEONARD EASY SONGS FOR MANDOLIN

MANDOLIN METHOD
Supplement to Any Mandolin Method

M000122018

Play the Melodies of 20 Pop, Bluegrass, Folk, Classical, and Blues Songs

BY RICH DELGROSSO

INTRODUCTION

Welcome to *Easy Songs for Mandolin*, a collection of 20 pop, bluegrass, folk, classical, and blues favorites arranged for easy mandolin. If you're a beginning mandolin player, you've come to the right place; these well-known songs will have you playing, reading, and enjoying music in no time!

This collection can be used on its own or as a supplement to the *Hal Leonard Mandolin Method – 2nd Edition* or any other beginning mandolin method. The songs are arranged in order of difficulty. Each melody is presented in an easy-to-read format—including extra mandolin parts and guitar chord symbols for your teacher or friend to play along. As you progress through the book, you can go back and try playing these other parts as well.

USING THE CD

Easy Songs for Mandolin is available as a book/CD package so you can practice playing with a real band. On the CD, each song begins with 2 full (or partial) measures of clicks, which sets the tempo and prepares you for playing along. To tune your mandolin to the CD, use the tuning notes on the final track (21).

ISBN 0-634-08739-8

HAL•LEONARD®
CORPORATION

7777 W. BLUEMOUND RD. P.O. BOX 13819 MILWAUKEE, WI 53213

Visit Hal Leonard Online at
www.halleonard.com

SONG STRUCTURE

The songs in this book have different sections, which may or may not include the following:

Intro
This is usually a short instrumental section that "introduces" the song at the beginning.

Verse
This is one of the main sections of a song and conveys most of the storyline. A song usually has several verses, all with the same music but each with different lyrics.

Chorus
This is often the most memorable section of a song. Unlike the verse, the chorus usually has the same lyrics every time it repeats.

Bridge
This section is a break from the rest of the song, often having a very different chord progression and feel.

Solo
This is an instrumental section, often played over the verse or chorus structure.

Outro
Similar to an intro, this section brings the song to an end.

ENDINGS & REPEATS

Many of the songs have some new symbols that you must understand before playing. Each of these represents a different type of ending.

1st and 2nd Endings
These are indicated by brackets and numbers. The first time through a song section, play the first ending and then repeat. The second time through, skip the first ending, and play through the second ending.

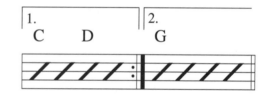

D.S.
This means "Dal Segno" or "from the sign." When you see this abbreviation above the staff, find the sign (𝄋) earlier in the song and resume playing from that point.

al Coda
This means "to the Coda," a concluding section in the song. If you see the words "D.S. al Coda," return to the sign (𝄋) earlier in the song and play until you see the words "To Coda," then skip to the Coda at the end of the song, indicated by the symbol: ⊕.

al Fine
This means "to the end." If you see the words "D.S. al Fine," return to the sign (𝄋) earlier in the song and play until you see the word "Fine."

D.C.
This means "Da Capo" or "from the head." When you see this abbreviation above the staff, return to the beginning (or "head") of the song and resume playing.

CONTENTS

PUFF THE MAGIC DRAGON

Words and Music by
LENNY LIPTON and PETER YARROW

LOVE ME TENDER

Words and Music by
ELVIS PRESLEY and VERA MATSON

EVERY BREATH YOU TAKE

Music and Lyrics by
STING

WHERE HAVE ALL THE FLOWERS GONE?

Words and Music by
PETE SEEGER

8

ALL MY LOVING

Words and Music by
JOHN LENNON and PAUL McCARTNEY

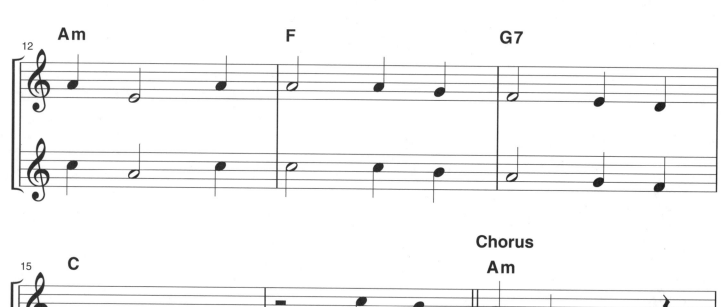

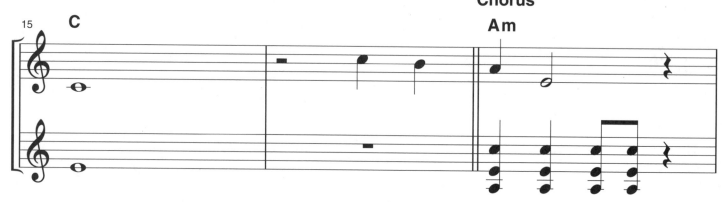

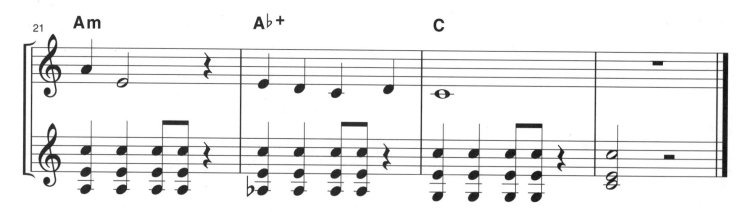

MAGGIE MAY

Words and Music by
ROD STEWART and MARTIN QUITTENTON

*Play 1st time only.

LET IT BE
(Duet)

Words and Music by
JOHN LENNON and PAUL McCARTNEY

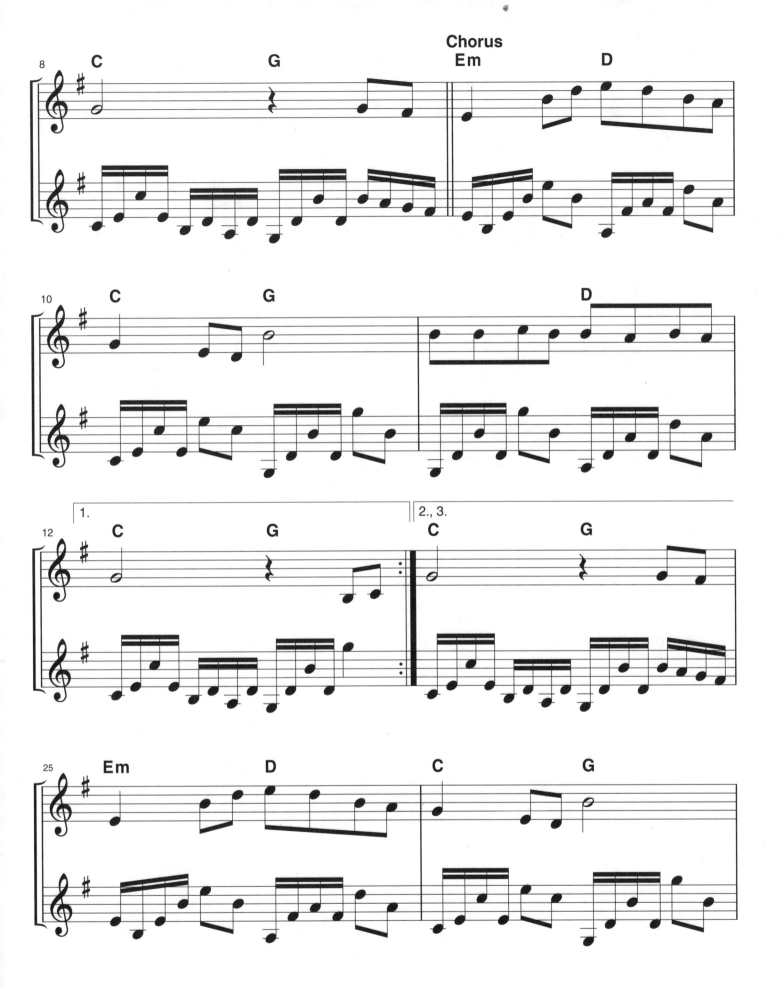

THE HOUSE OF THE RISING SUN

(Duet)

Words and Music by
ALAN PRICE

NORWEGIAN WOOD
(This Bird Has Flown)

Words and Music by
JOHN LENNON and PAUL McCARTNEY

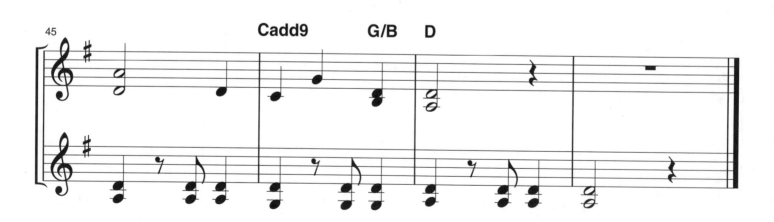

SCARBOROUGH FAIR
(Duet)

Traditional English

SOUTHWIND
(Celtic Air Solo)

Traditional

BABY PLEASE DON'T GO
(Blues Trio)

Words and Music by
JOSEPH LEE WILLIAMS

Swing feel
M.M. ♩ = 93

SANTA LUCIA
(Duet)

By TEODORO COTTRAU

TENNESSEE WALTZ
(Duet)

Words and Music by
REDD STEWART and PEE WEE KING

Chorus

CARELESS LOVE

Anonymous

ST. LOUIS BLUES
(Duet)

Words and Music by
W. C. HANDY

ANNIE'S SONG
(Duet)

Words and Music by
JOHN DENVER

CALIFORNIA DREAMIN'
(Duet)

Words and Music by
JOHN PHILLIPS and MICHELLE PHILLIPS

MUSETTE
(Duet)

By JOHANN SEBASTIAN BACH

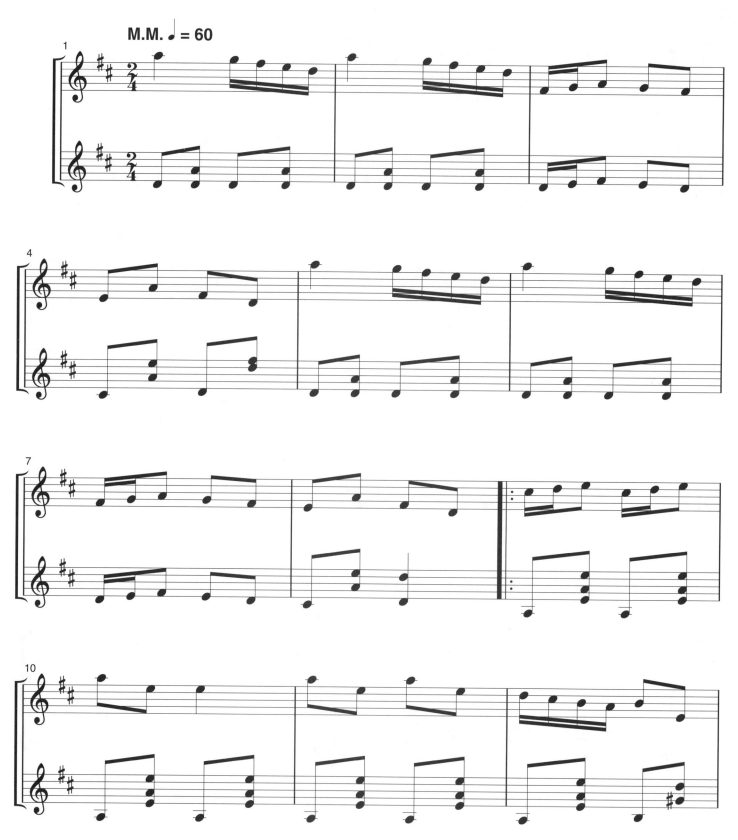

KEEP ON THE SUNNY SIDE

Words and Music by
A. P. CARTER

More Great Mandolin Publications

from

HAL•LEONARD®

HAL LEONARD MANDOLIN METHOD

Noted mandolinist and teacher Rich Del Grosso has authored this excellent mandolin method that features great playable tunes in several styles (bluegrass, country, folk, blues) in standard music notation and tablature. The optional audio features play-along duets.

00699296 Book Only...$6.95
00695102 Book/CD Pack...$14.95

CONTRUCTING A BLUEGRASS MANDOLIN

This beautifully detailed manual gives clear, step-by-step directions from raw materials to a magnificently finished mandolin through the use of simply-stated texts, photos and templates. Written by one of America's foremost authorities on acoustic instruments. 56 pages, spiral bound, including 19 full-sized blueprints covering each phase of construction. Also features a glossary of terms which enable the reader to more easily follow the instructions.

00699400 ....$16.95

FRETBOARD ROADMAPS – MANDOLIN

THE ESSENTIAL PATTERNS THAT ALL THE PROS KNOW AND USE
by Fred Sokolow and Bob Applebaum

The latest installment in our popular *Fretboard Roadmaps* series is a unique book/CD pack for all mandolin players. The CD includes 48 demonstration tracks for the exercises that will teach players to: play all over the fretboard, in any key; increase their chord, scale and lick vocabulary; play chord-based licks, moveable major and blues scales, first-position major scales and double stops; and more! Includes easy-to-follow diagrams and instructions for all levels of players.

00695357 Book/CD Pack...$12.95

MANDOLIN CHORD FINDER

EASY-TO-USE GUIDE TO OVER 1,000 MANDOLIN CHORDS
by Chad Johnson

Learn to play chords on the mandolin with this comprehensive, yet easy-to-use book. The *Hal Leonard Mandolin Chord Finder* contains over 1,000 chord diagrams for the most important 28 chord types, including three voicings for each chord. Also includes a lesson on chord construction, and a fingerboard chart of the mandolin neck!

00695739 9 X 12 Edition...$5.95

BILL MONROE – 16 GEMS

Authentic mandolin transcriptions of these classics by the Father of Bluegrass: Blue Grass Breakdown • Blue Grass Special • Can't You Hear Me Calling • Goodbye Old Pal • Heavy Traffic Ahead • I'm Going Back to Old Kentucky • It's Mighty Dark to Travel • Kentucky Waltz • Nobody Loves Me • Old Crossroad Is Waitin' • Remember the Cross • Shine Hallelujah Shine • Summertime Is Past and Gone • Sweetheart You Done Me Wrong • Travelin' This Lonesome Road • True Life Blues.

00690310 Mandolin Transcriptions $12.95

O BROTHER, WHERE ART THOU?

Perfect for beginning to advanced players, this collection contains both note-for-note transcribed mandolin solos, as well as mandolin arrangements of the melody lines for 11 songs from this Grammy-winning Album of the Year: Angel Band • The Big Rock Candy Mountain • Down to the River to Pray • I Am a Man of Constant Sorrow • I Am Weary (Let Me Rest) • I'll Fly Away • In the Highways (I'll Be Somewhere Working for My Lord) • In the Jailhouse Now • Indian War Whoop • Keep on the Sunny Side • You Are My Sunshine. Chord diagrams provided for each song match the chords from the original recording, and all songs are in their original key. Includes tab, lyrics and a mandolin notation legend.

00695762 ....$9.95

Learn to Play Mandolin!

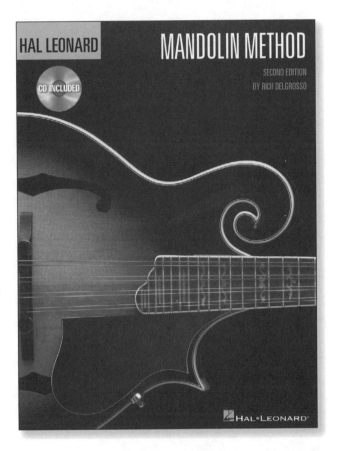

HAL LEONARD MANDOLIN METHOD

The *Hal Leonard Mandolin Method – Second Edition* is the newly updated and revised version of the original classic method by Rich DelGrosso. This comprehensive and easy-to-use beginner's guide includes many fun songs of different styles to learn and play. The accompanying CD includes 43 tracks of songs from the book for demonstration and play-along. You'll be playing mandolin in no time with the step-by-step instruction provided by this best-selling method. Book includes: Tips on Buying Instruments • Mandolin Anatomy • Instructions on Tuning • The Fundamentals of Music Reading • Music Notation and Tablature • Single-Note Picking • Chords, Scales, and Modes • Bluegrass Chops • Doublestops • Tremolo Picking • Drones • Bluegrass Songs • Songs from the United Kingdom • Old-Time Fiddle Tunes • Traditional Blues and Folk Songs • Classical Pieces • Solos and Duets • much more!

_____00699296 Book Only...$6.95
_____00695102 Book/CD Pack..$14.95

EASY SONGS FOR MANDOLIN – SUPPLEMENTARY SONGBOOK TO THE HAL LEONARD MANDOLIN METHOD

Play your favorite songs from The Beatles, James Taylor, The Carter Family, Pete Seeger, John Denver, The Mamas & the Papas, and more! Many musical styles are included, from folk to classical, pop to bluegrass, and beyond. The songs are presented in order of difficulty, beginning with easy rhythms and strum patterns and ending with songs that contain sixteenth notes and dotted rhythms.

_____00695865 Book Only...$6.95
_____00695866 Book/CD Pack..$14.95

MANDOLIN CHORD FINDER
EASY-TO-USE GUIDE TO OVER 1,000 MANDOLIN CHORDS
by Chad Johnson

Learn to play chords on the mandolin with this comprehensive, yet easy-to-use book. The *Hal Leonard Mandolin Chord Finder* contains over 1,000 chord diagrams for the most important 28 chord types, including three voicings for each chord. Also includes a lesson on chord construction, and a fingerboard chart of the mandolin neck!

_____00695740 6" x 9" Edition $5.95
_____00695739 9" x 12" Edition $6.95

MANDOLIN SCALE FINDER
EASY-TO-USE GUIDE TO OVER 1,300 MANDOLIN CHORDS
by Chad Johnson

Presents scale diagrams for the most often-used scales and modes in an orderly and easily accessible fashion. Use this book as a reference guide or as the foundation for creating an in-depth practice routine. Includes multiple patterns for each scale, a lesson on scale construction, and a fingerboard chart of the mandolin neck.

_____00695782 6" x 9" Edition $5.95
_____00695779 9" x 12" Edition $6.95

FOR MORE INFORMATION, SEE YOUR LOCAL MUSIC DEALER,
OR WRITE TO:

HAL•LEONARD®
CORPORATION
7777 W. BLUEMOUND RD. P.O. BOX 13819 MILWAUKEE, WI 53213

Visit Hal Leonard Online at
www.halleonard.com